MORGAN COUNTY PUBLIC LIBRARY
110 SOUTH JEFFERSON STREET
MARTINSVILLE, IN   46151

W9-AVK-620

J   Cobb, Mary.
746.44
COB   A sampler view of
           colonial life.

WITHDRAWN

10/2014

WITHDRAWN

A SAMPLER VIEW OF COLONIAL LIFE

A SAMPLER VIEW OF COLONIAL LIFE

∿ BY MARY COBB ∿

ILLUSTRATED BY JAN DAVEY ELLIS

THE MILLBROOK PRESS
BROOKFIELD, CONNECTICUT

For their love and support;
Kathy McIlvain, Charles Cobb,
Peggy Madden, Marilyn Cobb

Library of Congress Cataloging-in-Publication Data
Cobb, Mary.

A sampler view of colonial life: with projects kids can make / by Mary Cobb;
illustrated by Jan Davey Ellis.
p.   cm.
Summary: Describes the samplers stitched by girls in colonial America and explains what
these samplers tell about the lives of their makers. Includes simple projects.

ISBN 0-7613-0372-3 (lib. bdg).—ISBN 0-7613-0382-0 (pbk.)

1. Embroidery—Juvenile literature. 2. Embroidery—History—Juvenile literature.
3. Samplers—Juvenile literature. 4. Samplers—History—Juvenile literature.
5. United States—Social life and customs—To 1775—Juvenile literature. [1. Samplers—History.
2. Embroidery—History. 3. United States—Social life and customs—To 1775. 4. Handicraft.]
1. Ellis, Jan Davey, ill. II. Title.
TT770.5.C63   1999
746.44—dc21   98-2873   CIP   AC

Published by The Millbrook Press, Inc.
2 Old New Milford Road
Brookfield, Connecticut 06804

Text copyright © 1999 Mary Cobb
Illustrations copyright © 1999 Jan Davey Ellis
All rights reserved
Printed in the United States of America

hardcover: 5   4   3   2   1
paperback: 5   4   3   2   1

CONTENTS

A SAMPLER VIEW OF COLONIAL LIFE

WHAT IS A SAMPLER?

Look at the word *sampler*. Do you see that it contains the word *sample*? Have you ever had a sample of something—for example, ice cream? If you have, then you know that a sample is a little piece of a whole thing. Sometimes several related samples are grouped together. This is called a sampler.

From the early seventeenth to the late eighteenth century, the time known as the colonial period in American history, the women who came to this new land brought with them samples of embroidery patterns stitched onto narrow strips of cloth. These strips of cloth were called samplers.

Embroidery is a way of decorating and marking clothing and household materials with stitched patterns of colored thread. Today, you can find many beautiful embroidery stitches in sewing books. In the earliest days of our country, examples of pattern books for embroidery did not exist. When women visited one another they would bring along their sewing as well as these samplers of embroidery patterns to share. Later, at home, when a woman was ready to start a new sewing project, she could use her sampler of embroidery patterns as a source for ideas, much as an artist, when painting, uses a sketchbook to remember special scenes.

In colonial times, sewn samplers served another purpose for young girls. Sewing was an important and necessary skill that all girls had to learn. Making a sampler was a good way to learn, practice, and save examples of sewing stitches.

In colonial America, clothing and household materials not made at home could be purchased at stores. Because these items were imported from Europe, they were expensive to purchase or replace. It was a woman's job to see that the clothing, sheets, towels, and table linens that her family needed were kept in good repair. For this reason, rich or poor, colonial girls were taught to sew. If a family was poor, there would be little money to pay for a person to help with the sewing. A mother would be expected to do the sewing herself. If a family was well-to-do, a woman still had to be able to sew so she might teach and direct the family's servants and slaves as they worked on the family's sewing. The sampler was a young girl's workbook, a place to practice, improve, and save samples of her sewing skills.

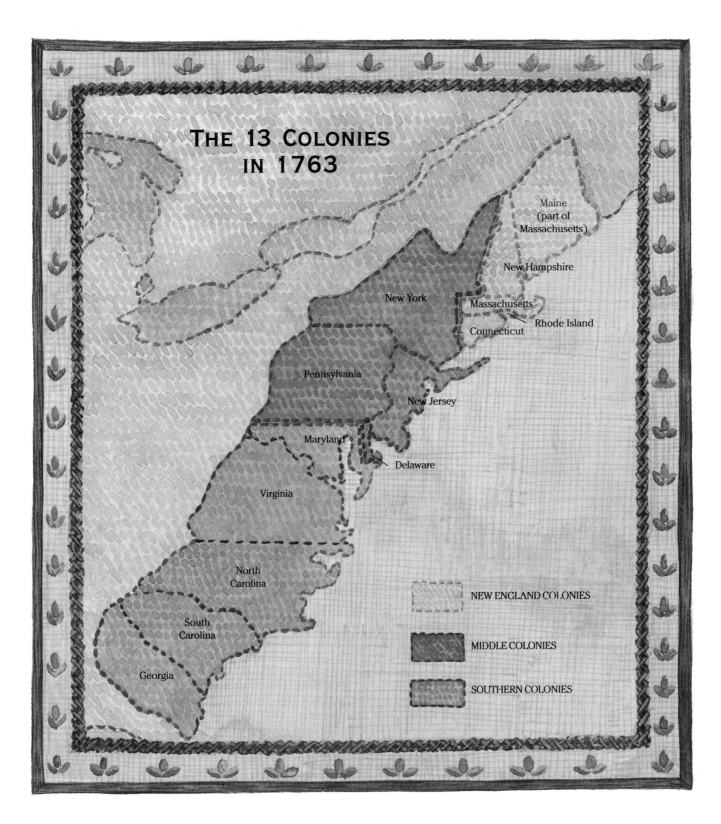

THE 13 COLONIES
IN 1763

Maine
(part of
Massachusetts)

New Hampshire

New York

Massachusetts

Rhode Island

Connecticut

Pennsylvania

New Jersey

Maryland

Delaware

Virginia

North
Carolina

South
Carolina

Georgia

NEW ENGLAND COLONIES

MIDDLE COLONIES

SOUTHERN COLONIES

Project:
A COLONIAL WALL POCKET

To store valuable papers, colonial women might sew an embroidered cloth pouch to hang on the wall. These cloth pouches, or wall pockets, served as a place to keep the family's papers, and they added color to a colonial room.

To make a wall pocket, trace the shape on medium-weight paper. Or you could enlarge the shape on a copy machine, or draw a larger version freehand. Cut out the pocket on the solid lines and fold on the dotted lines. Paste the tabs to the back of the pocket. With crayons or markers, decorate the wall pocket with your favorite designs. Hang your pocket on your bulletin board. Now you have a special place to store notes and cards.

✒ MAKING THE SAMPLER CLOTH ✒

For the most part, samplers were sewn on coarsely woven linen cloth made from the fibers of the flax plant. It took the colonial farmers many months of hard work to turn flax into linen. In the spring, after all danger from frost had passed, flaxseeds were sown in the fields. When the young flax plants were 3 to 4 inches (7.6 to 10 centimeters) high, women and children weeded the tender plants. After the flax plant had grown straight and tall, it was pulled up by the roots. The seedpods were broken off and saved for the next year's planting, and the flax stalks were spread out in the sun to dry.

Once dry, the stalks were tied into bundles and soaked in water for several weeks until the outer part had rotted away. The stalks were dried again, then crushed and beaten with a heavy club called a flax brake. This helped to separate the flax fibers from the hard outer bark of the plant. Finally, the women and girls combed the flax fibers through hackling combs until the fibers were soft and fine and ready to be spun into linen thread.

A spinning wheel was used to spin the combed fibers into linen thread. Some of the thread was saved for the family's sewing, but most of it was woven on looms into homespun linen cloth. The linen cloth was sewn into shirts and dresses, aprons and sheets. Leftover cloth scraps were saved for small projects such as samplers.

Other sewing samplers were stitched on woolen cloth made from sheep's fleece. In the spring, farmers sheared their sheep of their fleecy winter coats. This fleece was washed and cleaned of leaves, burs, and tangles. When the fleece had dried, it was pulled through carding combs to straighten the wool fibers. Using a spinning wheel, women spun the wool fiber into yarn that was used for knitting caps, stockings, and mittens as well as being woven into woolen cloth for the family's jackets and capes.

It took a lot of work on the part of the colonial family to produce the amount of homespun fabric they would need each year. Even the smallest piece of cloth was cherished and admired. A beautiful sampler not only brightened a home when hung on the wall for all to see but also served as a reminder of the skills needed to produce the materials.

PROJECT:
A WEAVING LOOM

A loom is a device for weaving threads or yarn into fabric. Looms for weaving fabric were large enough to fill an entire room. For this reason, looms were not usually set up in small houses. Instead, colonial families took their homespun yarn to a professional weaver to have it woven into material for clothing and household goods.

To make fabric, looms were threaded with a set of threads called the warp. The weaver then wove weft threads under and over the warp threads to produce cloth. Most homespun cloth was woven in the plain weave pattern, in which the weft thread is carried over all odd-numbered warp threads and under all even-numbered warp threads. In the next row, the weft thread passes over the even-numbered threads and under the odd-numbered threads. The plain weave pattern was the strongest and least complicated weave pattern to produce.

Try your hand at weaving. On medium-weight paper, make a copy of the weaving loom on page 18 and the weaving strips on page 19. Cut out as directed. Make slits in the weaving loom by cutting the black lines from dot to dot. Color the loom and strips, if desired. Weave the strips through the loom. Alternate the strips, weaving the first over and under and the next under and over, until you have filled the loom. Secure the weaving strips to the loom with glue or tape, then sign your weaving loom.

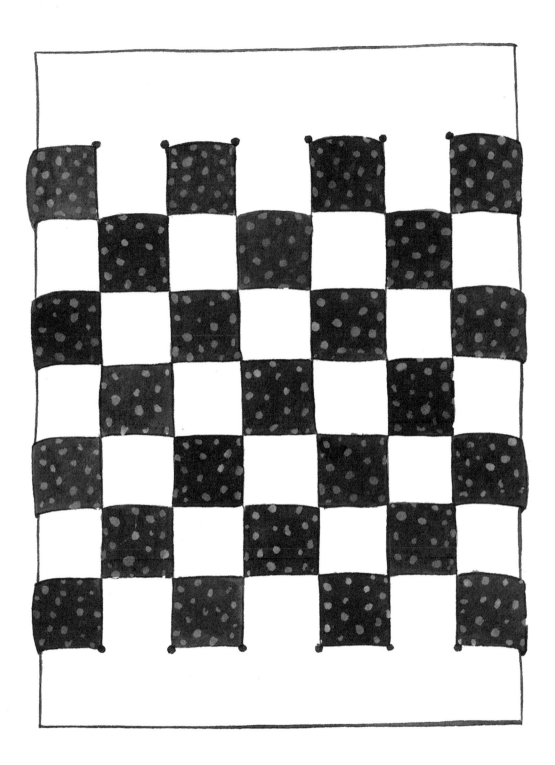

WEAVING LOOM

Name: _____

WEAVING STRIP PATTERN: MAKE SIX OR MORE

- -

- -

- -

- -

- -

- -

- -

∽ EMBROIDERY THREAD FOR SAMPLERS ∾

To embroider a sampler, you need colored thread. By the mid-eighteenth century, sailing ships from colonial America were trading with China for silk. Because silk thread was the same light, natural color as linen cloth, embroidery thread needed to be dyed to give it color to stand out and be seen.

Indigo blue and madder red were favorite dyes of the early colonists because they produced bright, permanent colors. Such dyes were expensive though, and had to be imported from Europe. So some colonial women began to use native leaves, flowers, berries, and nuts to produce inexpensive dyes. By experimenting, the women found that goldenrod blossoms yielded a lovely yellow; acorns, a dark brown; Queen Anne's lace flowers, a pretty green. Even American black oak bark yielded a highly prized golden-yellow dye.

But whatever the thread or dye, colonial families treasured their samplers stitched in rainbow hues.

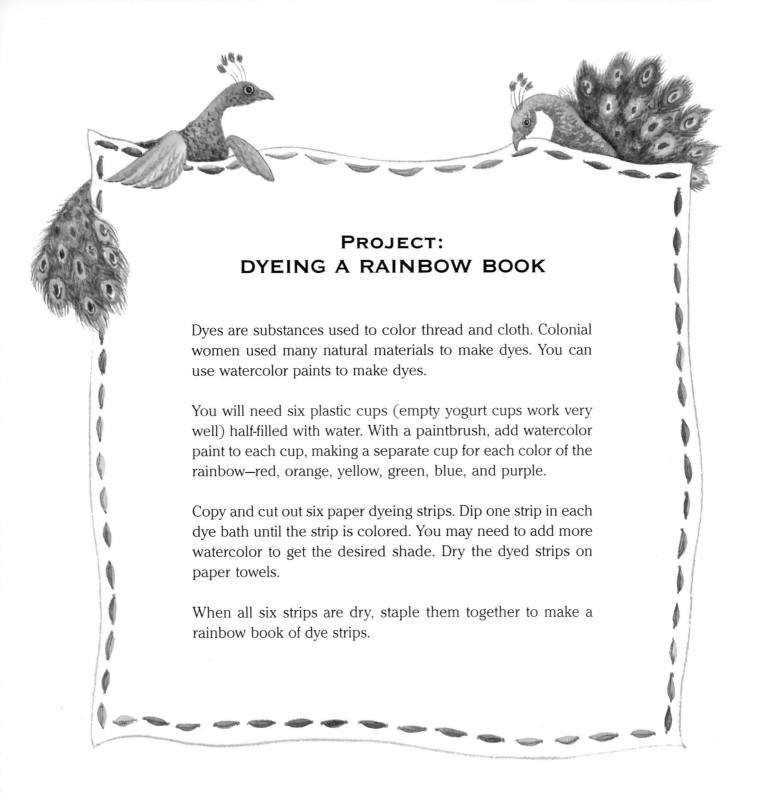

PROJECT:
DYEING A RAINBOW BOOK

Dyes are substances used to color thread and cloth. Colonial women used many natural materials to make dyes. You can use watercolor paints to make dyes.

You will need six plastic cups (empty yogurt cups work very well) half-filled with water. With a paintbrush, add watercolor paint to each cup, making a separate cup for each color of the rainbow—red, orange, yellow, green, blue, and purple.

Copy and cut out six paper dyeing strips. Dip one strip in each dye bath until the strip is colored. You may need to add more watercolor to get the desired shade. Dry the dyed strips on paper towels.

When all six strips are dry, staple them together to make a rainbow book of dye strips.

DYEING STRIPS: MAKE SIX OR MORE

✌ SAMPLER STITCHES ✌

The earliest samplers brought to America were long, narrow strips of fabric stitched with plain as well as fancy embroidery stitches. These narrow samplers were usually rolled up and stored in a woman's sewing basket, to be referred to later to share a particular stitch pattern with family or friends.

By the mid-eighteenth century, most women owned sewing samplers they had made as children. Pattern books began arriving from Europe. Now sampler making became part of a girl's education, a way to practice her sewing skills. Fancy, intricate stitches disappeared from samplers as schoolgirls stitched alphabets, numerals, and verses onto their marking samplers using the simple cross-stitch, or sampler stitch. The shape of samplers also changed from long and narrow to wider and shorter, like book pages.

By 1800, the simple cross-stitched alphabet samplers changed again to elaborately embroidered samplers. Although girls were still taught the simple cross-stitch, they also learned the satin, back, queen's, tent, rope, and buttonhole stitches and embellished their samplers with them.

❧ SAMPLER STITCHES ❧

cross stitch

queen stitch

rope stitch

tent stitch

satin stitch

back stitch

buttonhole stitch

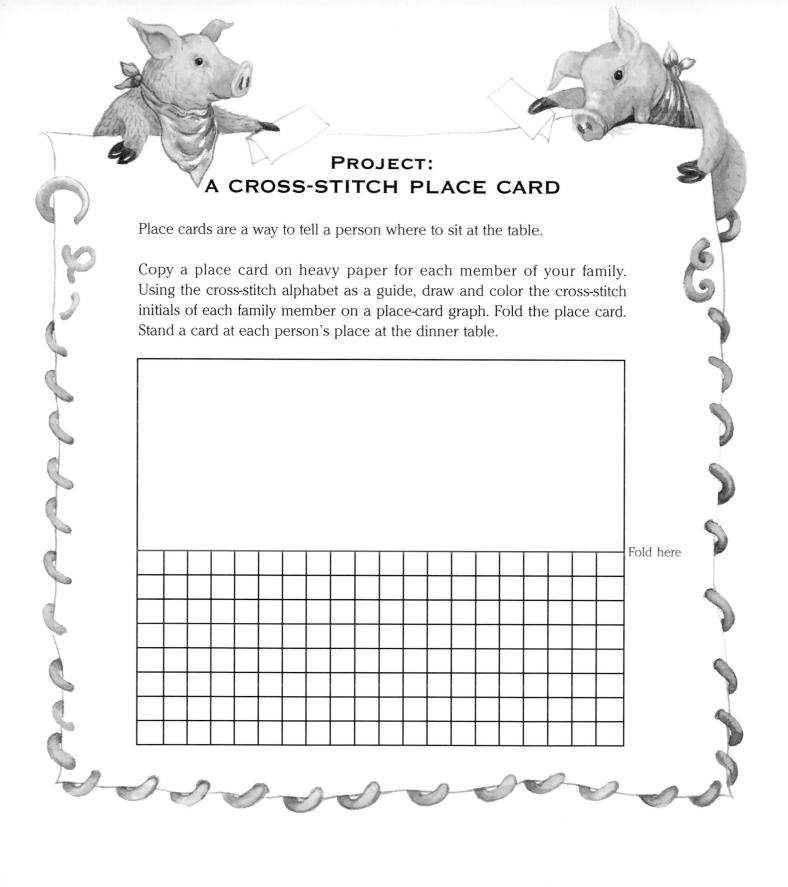

PROJECT:
A CROSS-STITCH PLACE CARD

Place cards are a way to tell a person where to sit at the table.

Copy a place card on heavy paper for each member of your family. Using the cross-stitch alphabet as a guide, draw and color the cross-stitch initials of each family member on a place-card graph. Fold the place card. Stand a card at each person's place at the dinner table.

Fold here

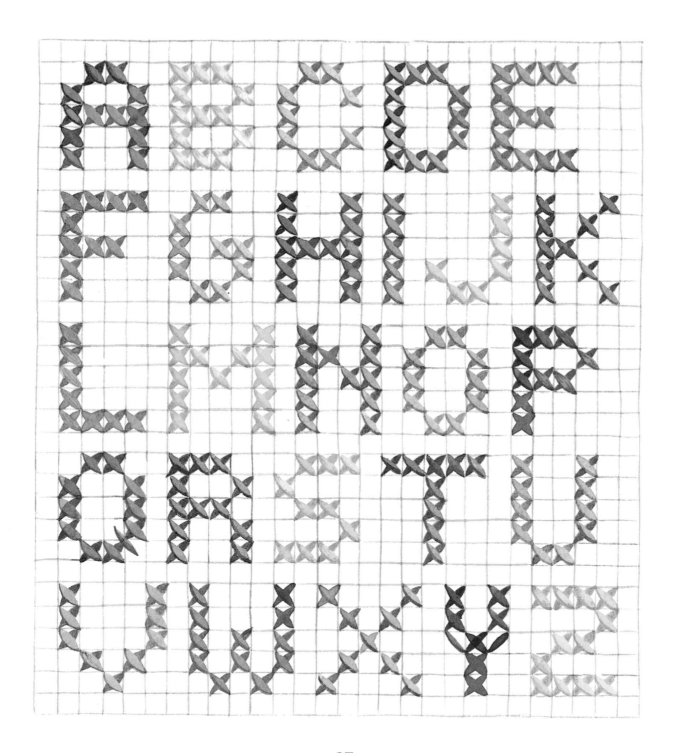

∽ THE SAMPLER AND ITS DESIGN ∾

The first samplers in early America did not have fixed designs, and samplers changed over the years as the sampler makers added new rows of needlework. By 1750, the purpose and design of samplers had changed. Instead of a place to store embroidery patterns, samplers were now made as part of a schoolgirl's academic as well as her domestic education. The design of a schoolgirl's sampler usually included an alphabet, numerals, perhaps a verse, the sampler maker's name, and a date when the sampler had been completed. If there was room at the bottom edge of the sampler cloth, the sewer might embroider a special picture.

Scenes from the Bible were popular with sampler makers. Adam and Eve and the serpent in the Garden of Eden and the Tree of Life were often pictured. Others embroidered pictures of birds, animals, flowers, trees, and houses onto their needlework designs. In the early days of this country, winter was a terrible time. Houses were cold and drafty, and feet and fingers were often frozen. Spring was a season of warmth, a happier time. Perhaps that is why so many sampler makers chose to picture warm, happy spring scenes on their samplers.

By the late eighteenth century, America had won its independence from Great Britain and become a separate nation. George Washington was chosen to serve as the first president of the United States of America. Samplers made at that time often included a picture of the first president. The American flag, Liberty Bell, and Independence Hall, all symbols of this new nation, found their way into sampler designs.

To finish a sampler, an embroidered border was hand-stitched around its edges. A border served to frame the sampler. Designs for borders might be geometrical or elaborate pictures of vines and flowers. A well-sewn sampler was highly prized. Proud families had the samplers framed and displayed them in a prominent place in their homes for visitors to admire. Samplers were bright, colorful decorations, a way for a girl to show off her schooling and her sewing accomplishments.

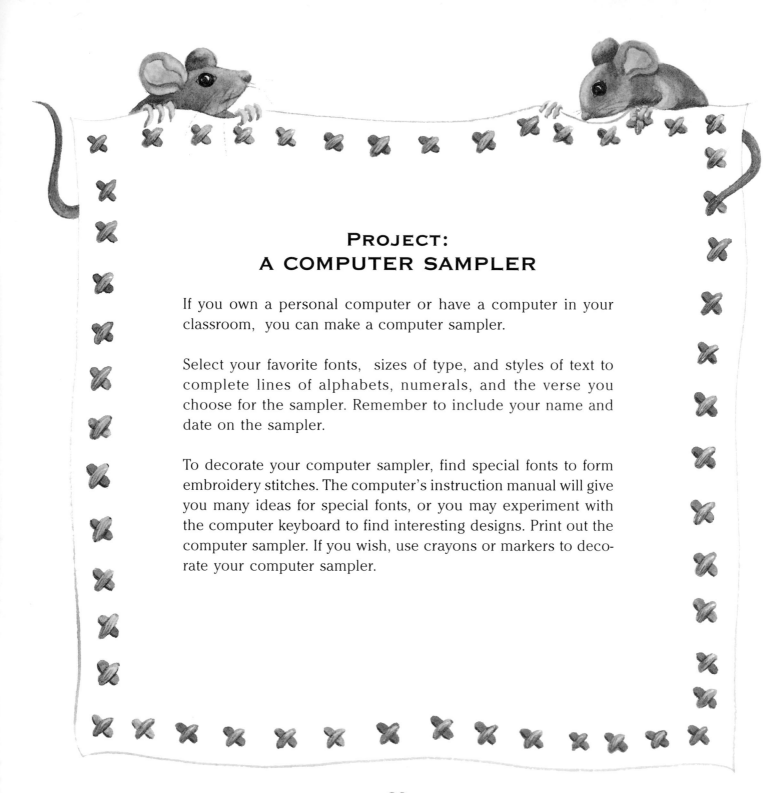

Project:
A COMPUTER SAMPLER

If you own a personal computer or have a computer in your classroom, you can make a computer sampler.

Select your favorite fonts, sizes of type, and styles of text to complete lines of alphabets, numerals, and the verse you choose for the sampler. Remember to include your name and date on the sampler.

To decorate your computer sampler, find special fonts to form embroidery stitches. The computer's instruction manual will give you many ideas for special fonts, or you may experiment with the computer keyboard to find interesting designs. Print out the computer sampler. If you wish, use crayons or markers to decorate your computer sampler.

* * * * * * * * * * *

A B C D E F G H
I J K L M N O P Q R
S T U V W X Y Z

* * * * * * * * * * *

a b c d e f g h i
j k l m n o p
q r s t u v w x y z

* * * * * * * * * * *

Julie Pratt is my name
And with my computer
I wrought the same.

January 31, 1999

⌐ SAMPLER VERSES AND INSCRIPTIONS ⌐

Sampler verses were a special part of a girl's sampler. The youngest sewers chose simple rhymes. A five-year-old girl embroidered: "Mary Smith is my name and with my nedel I wrought the same."

Other young sampler makers chose equally simple verses.

Here is my sampler,
Here you see
What care my mother
Took of me.

or

When I was young and in my prime
Here you may see how I spent my time.

Older girls would choose more elaborate verses. Passages from the Bible were often used, as most families owned that book. Other sampler makers might select a poem on virtue, humility, selflessness, or death. Sometimes a particular sampler verse was a family tradition. A girl might be expected to use a verse once used by her mother, aunt, or grandmother.

Though life is fair
And pleasure young
And Love on ev'ry
Shepherd's tongue,
I turn my thoughts
To serious things
Life is ever on the wing.

Sampler verses tell us that not all girls enjoyed making a sampler. Patty Polk hated sewing, and she had enough spunk to say so. On her sampler, she stitched: "Patty Polk did this and she hated every stitch she did in it. She loves to read much more."

Another girl tried very hard to make a beautiful sampler, but despite her efforts, her stitching just never seemed to come out right. We know this because on her sampler she stitched: "Hannah Fisher is my name, And with my needle I wrought the same, And if my skill had been better, I would have mended every letter."

A Vermont schoolgirl found that she loved working on her sampler so much that on Saturday nights she hid it far beneath the largest bed in the house. Sewing on the Sabbath day was forbidden, and she knew if she saw her sampler, she would be tempted to put away her catechism and Bible lessons and begin stitching.

Making a sampler was an expected and sometimes entire part of a girl's formal education. However, many parents knew the importance of education and wanted much more for their daughters. Perhaps that is why this verse so often appears on samplers.

Labor for learning before thou art old
For learning is better than silver and gold.
For silver and gold will vanish away
But learning is a jewel that will never decay.

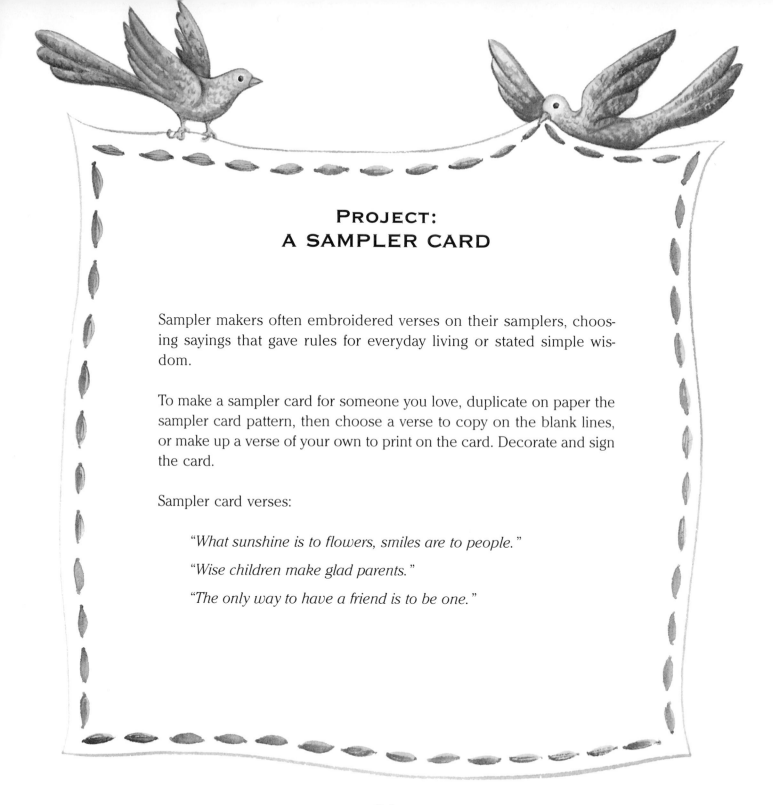

Project:
A SAMPLER CARD

Sampler makers often embroidered verses on their samplers, choosing sayings that gave rules for everyday living or stated simple wisdom.

To make a sampler card for someone you love, duplicate on paper the sampler card pattern, then choose a verse to copy on the blank lines, or make up a verse of your own to print on the card. Decorate and sign the card.

Sampler card verses:

"What sunshine is to flowers, smiles are to people."

"Wise children make glad parents."

"The only way to have a friend is to be one."

ABCDEFGHIJKLMNOPQRSTUVWXYZ

abcdefghijklmnopqrstuvwxyz

  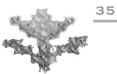   

∽: A SAMPLER FRAME :∼

In the eighteenth century, a schoolchild's marking sampler was tucked away to be referred to when a girl had forgotten how to cross-stitch letters and numbers. By the nineteenth century, as a little girl learned to sew, she still might make a simple marking sampler for her sewing box; then, after she had perfected her sewing skills, she made an ornate sampler for display. Families took great pride in displaying these colorful samplers, but because their nineteenth-century homes were often cold and damp, and smoke from fireplaces and burning candles darkened the walls, a beautiful sampler would need to be framed to protect it from soot and dampness.

At first, wooden sampler frames were expensive and had to be ordered from a cabinetmaker. Other samplers were sewn to a stiff piece of pasteboard and then covered with glass and hung on the wall for all to see.

By the nineteenth century, framing shops had opened in many towns and cities. Samplers, completed at girls' education academies, could be taken to a shop and framed at a reasonable cost.

SAMPLER MAKING AND SCHOOLS

⌣ DAME SCHOOLS AND A MARKING SAMPLER ⌢

In the earliest days of America, there were no schools. Children whose parents could spare the time from work were taught to read and write at home. The colonists wanted more for their children: They wanted them to be able to read the Bible as well as to read and understand the laws of this new land. Community leaders voted to arrange for schooling for the children. These leaders also believed that not only should children be taught to read and write but each boy and girl should learn some kind of useful work at school. Sewing was important work, and it was a skill that a child would have to master. Sewing could be taught at school.

Before 1750, the first school in many towns was the dame school. It was held in a private home, usually the teacher's house. For a small fee, boys and girls, from age three to eight, could attend dame school. There, the pupils took turns reciting the ABC's, the numerals, and simple prayers.

There were no books, paper, or pencils at a dame school. At a dame school, the children might use a hornbook as a pattern for the alphabet and numbers they stitched onto their marking samplers. A hornbook was a flat piece of wood covered with a sheet of paper printed with the alphabet and numerals. To save the paper from wear and tear, it was covered with a transparent slice of animal horn attached to the wood with brass nails. Other children might use a "battledore" to learn their letters and numbers. A battledore was a folded card printed with the alphabet, numbers, small pictures, and rhymes. Because a battledore cost only a penny, families might purchase one for their children. Hornbooks and battledores were used to teach children letters and numbers and also often served as patterns for marking samplers.

While the teacher was busy with one group of children, others practiced their work skills. With homespun cloth, needle, and thread, girls worked on a marking sampler. To make a marking sampler, an older student would teach the beginner sewer how to cross-stitch the letters of the alphabet, the numerals, and the student's name on a strip of cloth. At home it was the children's job to mark or cross-stitch the family's name on all the clothing and linens the family owned. A cross-stitch marking sampler was handy to have at home for remembering the ABC's and the numbers.

Because dame schools were not free, children whose parents could not afford to pay tuition did not attend school. Children who did not live within walking distance of the school could not go to school. Some parents chose not to send their children to school at all. A dame school teacher might close the school for many weeks during the winter or if she had household work that needed attention. For these reasons, many dame schools were open only four or five weeks out of each year.

By the end of the eighteenth century, laws were passed requiring communities with more than fifty children to build schoolhouses and hire schoolmasters to teach the children reading, handwriting, and arithmetic. Usually, these schools consisted of one room and were known as district schools.

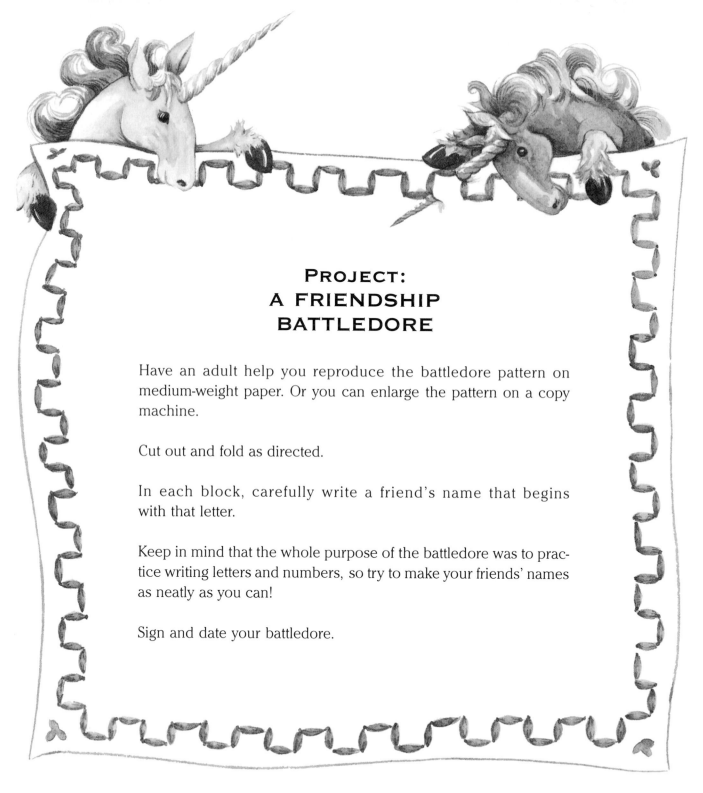

Project:
A FRIENDSHIP
BATTLEDORE

Have an adult help you reproduce the battledore pattern on medium-weight paper. Or you can enlarge the pattern on a copy machine.

Cut out and fold as directed.

In each block, carefully write a friend's name that begins with that letter.

Keep in mind that the whole purpose of the battledore was to practice writing letters and numbers, so try to make your friends' names as neatly as you can!

Sign and date your battledore.

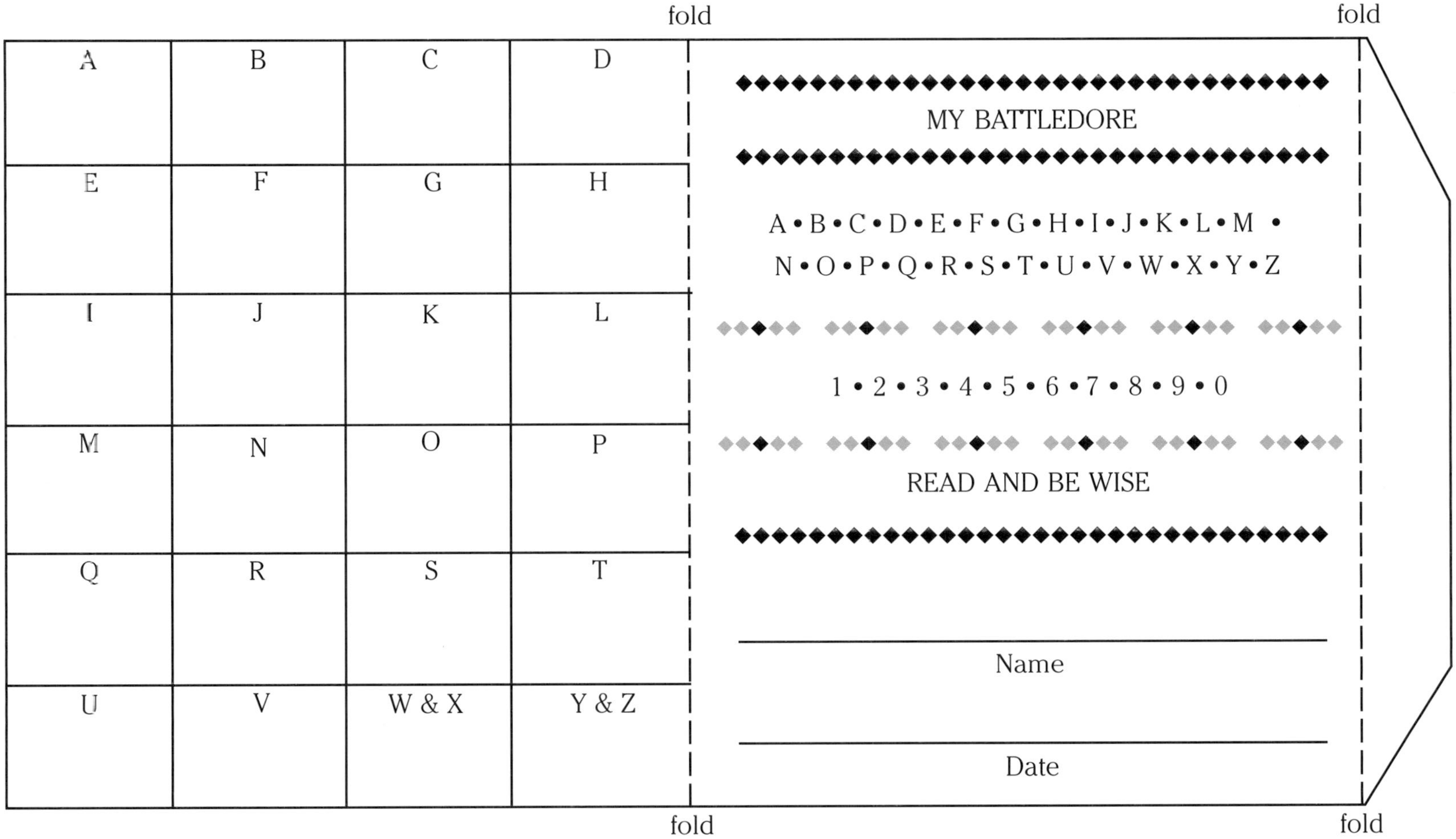

fold

MY BATTLEDORE

A • B • C • D • E • F • G • H • I • J • K • L • M •
N • O • P • Q • R • S • T • U • V • W • X • Y • Z

1 • 2 • 3 • 4 • 5 • 6 • 7 • 8 • 9 • 0

READ AND BE WISE

Name

Date

fold

A	B	C	D
E	F	G	H
I	J	K	L
M	N	O	P
Q	R	S	T
U	V	W & X	Y & Z

·: DISTRICT SCHOOLS :·

The district schoolhouse was usually located in the center of the community. Children of all ages were crowded together into one room and taught by one teacher, the schoolmaster. A district school was usually opened for two terms each year, a nine-week winter term and a six-week summer term. Early in the eighteenth century, only boys were allowed to enroll in a district school. But by the middle of the eighteenth century, if the teacher was a woman, girls might attend the school's summer term.

As in the dame schools, children attending district schools were required to bring their own school supplies. Children brought homemade copybooks, ink, and quill pens from home. Some children brought slates and pieces of chalk to use when they practiced handwriting. Families were expected to furnish their children's books. Many families owned a primer, a book for beginning readers, as well as a spelling book, and the children brought these to school. Other children brought the Bible to use as their reading book. Besides learning the three R's—reading, writing, and arithmetic—district-school students were taught to listen, stand up when spoken to, and in all ways be mannerly and respectful. Students who broke school rules were often punished severely.

In the eighteenth century, the district school was the only school that many children ever attended. No child ever graduated or received a diploma from a district school. School ended when the parents thought the child had received enough education, or for others, school ended when the children were needed to work at home. Even so, nearly every boy eventually learned to read and write and to do enough mathematics to keep the family's account books.

After leaving a district school, if a family was well-to-do, a boy would be sent to a private academy for further schooling. At an academy, boys were taught Greek, Latin, history, geography, mathematics, composition, and literature. Boys who did well at an academy could go on to college.

Sadly, very few girls ever attended a district school long enough to learn to read or to complete even the simplest of marking samplers. In the eighteenth century, girls were not expected to excel in learning but to marry and raise families. Academies and colleges were not open to women. However, some well-to-do families who wanted more education for their daughters might send them to private schools, known as seminaries, for young ladies.

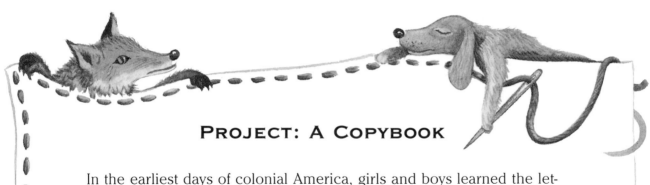

PROJECT: A COPYBOOK

In the earliest days of colonial America, girls and boys learned the letters of the alphabet with a hornbook or battledore. Later, paper was manufactured in this country, and children practiced their handwriting in homemade copybooks.

Copybooks were made at home. First, a sheet of paper was cut in half, and the halves were folded together to make a booklet of four pages. A piece of coarse brown wrapping paper was cut to size to make a cover for the copybook. Then, with needle and thread, the book was sewn together at the middle seam.

At school, the boys and girls ruled the pages of their homemade copybooks with a straight edge and a piece of lead called a plummet. Then the schoolmaster would write a sentence on the first line of the page. Using ink and a quill pen, a student was expected to copy that sentence on each remaining line of the copybook page exactly as the teacher had written it.

Teachers chose copy sentences that taught proper manners, prayers, or good behavior. Later, copy sentences were devised that contained each letter of the alphabet. In that way, children could practice all the letters of the alphabet in one sentence.

Here is such a copy sentence:

"A quiet frog jumps when vexed by lazy ducks."

To make your own copybook, staple together several pieces of lined paper. Write the copy sentence at the top of the first page of your copybook. Practice your handwriting by copying the sentence. Perhaps you can think up your own copy sentence. Write that sentence in your copybook. When George Washington, the first president of the United States, was a student, he made his own copybooks. A number of them were saved and are on display at Mount Vernon, Washington's home in Virginia.

a quick brown fox jumps over the lazy dog.
a quick brown fox jumps over the lazy dog.
a quick brown fox jumps over the lazy dog.

◡: THE SEMINARY AND SAMPLERS :◡

By 1770, academies or seminaries for girls had been established in many cities and larger towns along the Atlantic seaboard. The purpose of these schools was to give girls aged nine to sixteen a chance to further their education beyond the district school. A girl's attendance at these schools depended very much on her family's wealth and their attitude toward education.

The academies promised to turn their students into "finished" young ladies, ready to be presented to society. The schools taught reading, writing, arithmetic, geography, and needlework, as well as music and dancing. Many schools advertised: "Each young lady will have a framed piece, a sampler, on her return home to present to her parents." For that reason, a large part of each school day was taken up learning sewing and embroidery skills.

Virtue and proper deportment were emphasized at finishing school. Girls learned to listen, and be obedient, graceful, and quiet. When studying or sewing, the girls were required to sit with back straight and head held high.

As a reminder to sit or stand correctly, students wore undergarments fitted with thin strips of metal or wood to help with correct posture.

Academy samplers were much different from the simple marking samplers completed at a dame school. The academy samplers were more nearly square in shape and elaborately embroidered with alphabets, numbers, verses, pictures, and borders. Elegant embellishments were added to these samplers. Silk thread, human hair, ribbons, paint, and paper were used to enhance the samplers. If a girl could not draw a design, an artist might be hired to draw the pictures on her sampler.

Samplers from the same academy tended to be similar in appearance, for each school developed a unique pattern for their students to use.

PROJECT:
REWARDS OF MERIT

Academies and boarding schools often gave deserving students Rewards of Merit. If a girl worked diligently at her academic or her sewing skills, she might earn such an award. Good manners were also rewarded.

A Reward of Merit was highly prized and displayed in the student's home in a place of honor.

Ask an adult to help you copy this Reward of Merit. Think of a person who might deserve a reward. Print that person's name on the award. Sign, date, and decorate the award. Present the award with a big smile and hug.

* *

REWARD OF MERIT

This certifies that _____
*by hard work and good behavior has earned the praise
of family and friends.*

_____

Date: _____

* *

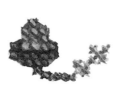

SPECIAL SAMPLERS

Although simple marking samplers and academy-school samplers were the kind most often completed by children, other samplers were made as well. To demonstrate their ability at handwriting, students attending district schools created special handwriting samplers from parchment paper using ink and quill pens. Because homemade ink tended to fade quickly, only a few of these paper samplers ever survived. Those that have are usually found in museums.

As part of their education and to show their skill at repairing fabrics, some finishing schools required their students to make a darning/weaving sampler. It took many hours of hard work to sew enough clothing for a family's needs. If an item of clothing had worn spots or was accidentally torn, it would not be discarded. Instead, the damaged and worn spots were carefully mended by darning or weaving threads across the tears in the fabric. Some girls took great pride in their darning and weaving skills, repairing the family's clothing so that the darned spots were invisible. Other girls hated the task. In large and small families, girls found little time to play, for there was always a basket of mending awaiting their attention.

A map or geography sampler might be completed as part of a girl's study of geography, the study of the Earth's surface. Map or geography samplers were usually sewn on imported silk cloth and embroidered with beautifully dyed silk thread. Some girls chose to embroider the map of Europe, while others hand-stitched maps of America. Because the maps available to students were not always accurate, a geography sampler was not always an accurate chart of an area.

Some finishing-school students made genealogy samplers. Along with the embroidered rows of alphabets and pictures, the sampler maker would stitch the name and date of birth of each family member. Making a genealogy sampler was an ongoing process. As the family grew, new names were added to the sampler; if a family member died, that date would be stitched onto the sampler. In a few cases, the date of death of the sampler maker herself was stitched on by a surviving family member.

Some academies required their students to complete a sewing sampler. Girls were expected to learn many sewing skills. To construct her family's clothing, she would need to know how to sew a seam, hem a garment, make buttonholes, and sew on buttons. To show her skill in each of these areas, girls were required to produce a sampler showing these techniques. In some schools, girls were also taught a catechism of sewing and had to memorize and be ready to answer many questions concerning hand sewing. Few sewing samplers survive today, mostly because sewing samplers were not colorfully embroidered and seldom framed and displayed.

At the close of a district school's term, the older students often prepared a special paper sampler to show their skills at handwriting. Like the cloth sampler, paper samplers called exhibition pieces were highly prized. Exhibition pieces included alphabets and numerals, as well as a sentence or two. Happiness, friendship, and patriotism were often the subjects chosen for exhibition-piece sentences. Much like the cloth sampler, the exhibition piece would have a decorative border and drawings of birds, flowers, houses, and trees. Finally, the exhibition piece was signed and dated.

Preparing a handwriting exhibition piece was not easy. First the pointed end of a goose feather would be sharpened to make a quill pen. A sheet of paper called foolscap had to be purchased from a store. The foolscap was rubbed with gum arabic powder so that it would be able to absorb ink.

Families who lived near a city could purchase ink powder from stores, but farm families might use natural materials to make ink. Black ink could be made from the bark of the swamp maple tree. The bark was gathered and then boiled in an iron kettle to give the ink a deep dark color. Homemade ink was often weak and pale. Over time, the handwriting in copybooks and on exhibition pieces completed with homemade ink tended to fade away.

PROJECT:
A HANDWRITING SAMPLER

To make a handwriting sampler, you will need a copy of the blank exhibition piece. In your best handwriting, copy the following sentence on the lines of the exhibition piece.

"The only way to have a friend is to be a friend."

Sign, decorate, and share your exhibition piece with your family. Exhibition pieces make wonderful presents for grandparents.

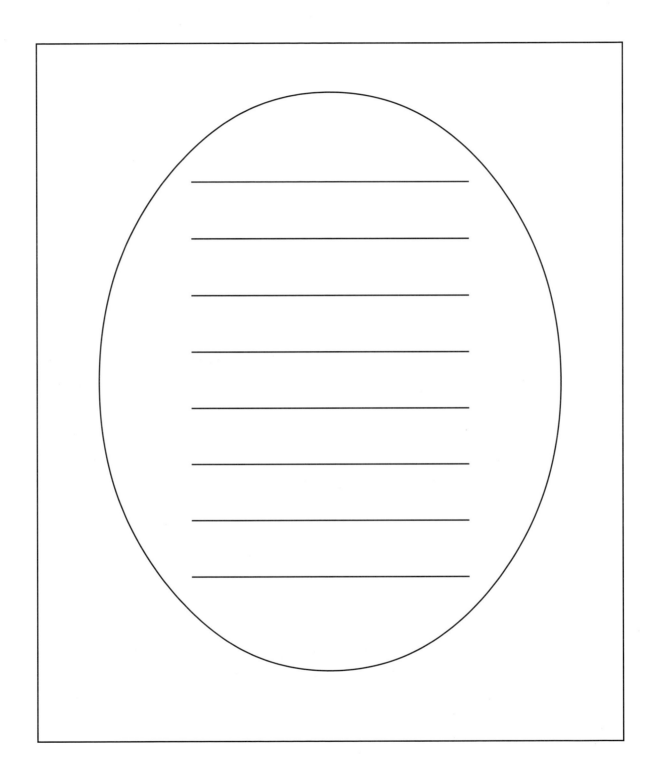

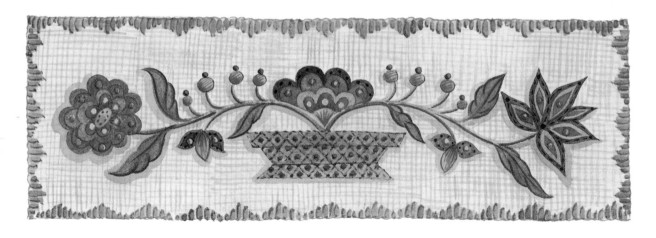

WHAT WE CAN LEARN
FROM SAMPLERS

From the mid-seventeenth to the mid-nineteenth century, young girls received very little in the way of education in this country. A large part of their education was through sampler making. By studying old samplers, we know that girls not only practiced exercises in stitchery but also learned the alphabet and numerals. The hand-stitched sampler verses show that they learned to read and spell. In the early days of this country, birthdays were not celebrated as they are today. What is more, the birth of a baby girl might not have been recorded by name in a town's annual census. Because many samplers were signed and dated, today we have documentation of these girls' existence.

Education for girls changed during the nineteenth century. America's leaders and educators agreed that this would be a greater nation if both boys and girls had equal opportunities to be educated. By 1840, state legislatures began enacting laws that allowed girls to attend high school. Some colleges opened their doors to young women. Textile mills were set up that wove woolen, cotton, and linen cloth. Clothing was manufactured in factories. Marking a family's clothing with colored thread became unnecessary when indelible marking ink was invented. Learning needlework was no longer the most important part of a school's curriculum. Sampler making was put aside.

Today, samplers stitched by colonial schoolgirls are cherished heirlooms and can be found in museums, private collections, and the homes of the sampler makers' descendants. Scholars research, photograph, and record the existence of old samplers, and books are published showing these samplers. Old samplers are much sought after by collectors.

Now sampler making has become a popular hobby. The materials for making a sampler are available at many craft and fabric stores. Perhaps you have a cross-stitched sampler in your home or have seen one in a friend's house. When you look at a sampler, remember that long ago a sampler was not only an exercise in stitchery and a demonstration of needlework skills but it was a colonial girl's workbook.

Project:
A Nowadays Sampler

Long ago in our country, young girls made marking samplers as part of their education. Making a sampler was a way to learn sewing skills as well as to practice making letters and numbers. Nowadays boys and girls use paper and pencils, books, and computers to help them learn to read. Sewing skills are usually taught at home or in junior and senior high schools.

Perhaps, as you have read about samplers, you have wanted to make a sampler of your own. Try this easy-to-stitch Nowadays sampler. For your sampler, you will need a 14-inch (36-centimeter) square of medium-weight cotton muslin material, embroidery thread, scissors, a pencil, and a needle with a large eye.

With your pencil, lightly sketch the Nowadays sampler pattern onto the cloth material (or make up a sampler design of your own). Thread the needle with embroidery thread, and knot one end of the thread. Work the running stitch over the — lines of your design. When you have finished your sampler, display it on a wall or bulletin board.

THE RUNNING STITCH
To complete a running stitch, bring the threaded needle up through the cloth at the beginning of a — and down through the cloth at the end of a —. When you have completed a row of running stitches, make several tiny stitches on the back of the cloth to secure the thread.

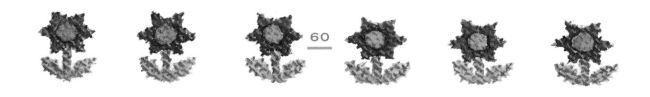

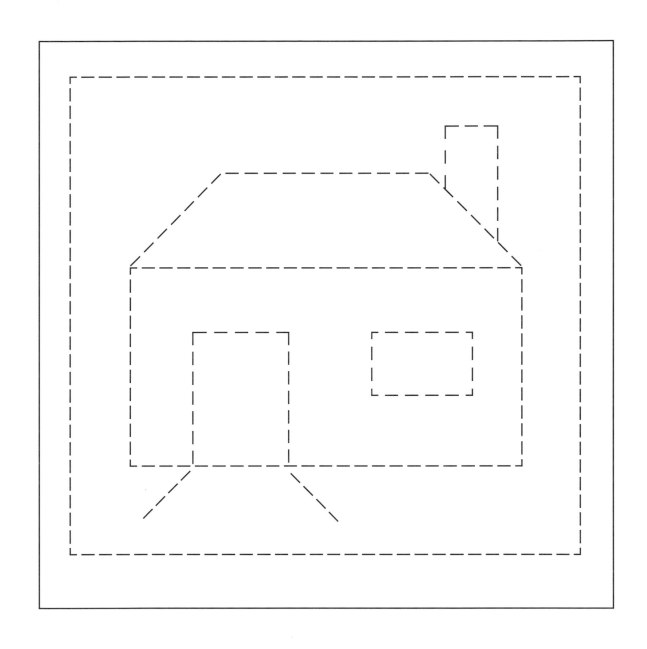

  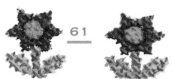

BIBLIOGRAPHY

SAMPLERS

Bolton, Ethel. *American Samplers*. New York: Dover Publications, 1973.

Christie, Mrs. Archibald H. *Samplers & Stitches*. Great Neck, NY: Hearthside Press, 1971.

Colby, Averil. *Samplers*. London: B.T. Batsford, 1984.

Edmonds, Mary Jaene. *Samplers and Samplermakers*. New York: Rizzoli, 1991.

Grow, Judith K. *Creating Historic Samplers*. Princeton, NJ: Pyne Press, 1974.

Krueger, Glee E. *New England Samplers to 1840*. Sturbridge, MA: Old Sturbridge Village, 1978.

Rettew, Gayle A. *Behold The Labour of My Tender Age*. Rochester, NY: Rochester Museum & Science Center, 1983.

Ryan, Patricia, and Allen D. Bragdon. *Historic Samplers*. Boston: Little, Brown & Co., 1992.

Swan, Susan Burrows. *Plain and Fancy: American Women and Their Needlework 1700-1850*. New York: Holt, Rinehard and Winston, 1977.

SCHOOLING AND EDUCATION

Earle, Alice Morse. *Child Life in Colonial Days*. Bowie, MD: Heritage Books, 1992.

——. *Customs and Fashions in Old New England*. Bowie, MD: Heritage Books, 1992.

Larkin, Jack. *Children Everywhere*. Sturbridge, MA: Old Sturbridge Village, 1987.

INDEX